A Painful History of Medicine

Pox, Pus & Plague

a history of disease and infection

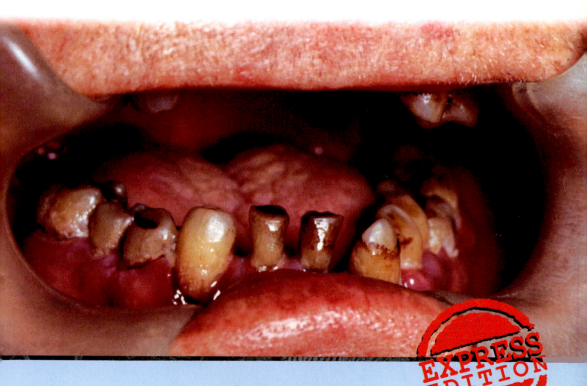

John Townsend

www.raintreepublishers.co.uk

Visit our website to find out more information about **Raintree** books.

To order:
- ☎ Phone 44 (0) 1865 888113
- 🖹 Send a fax to 44 (0) 1865 314091
- 💻 Visit the Raintree bookshop at **www.raintreepublishers.co.uk** to browse our catalogue and order online.

First published in Great Britain by Raintree,
Halley Court, Jordan Hill, Oxford OX2 8EJ,
part of Harcourt Education.
Raintree is a registered trademark
of Harcourt Education Ltd.

© Harcourt Education Ltd 2006
First published in paperback in 2006
The moral right of the proprietor has
been asserted.

Editorial: Carol Usher, Melanie Copland,
and Kate Buckingham
Design: Michelle Lisseter, Rob Norridge,
and Bridge Creative Services Ltd
Picture Research: Hannah Taylor
and Ginny Stroud-Lewis
Production: Duncan Gilbert
Originated by Dot Gradations
Printed and bound in China
by South China Printing Company

ISBN 1 406 20430 7 (hardback)
10 09 08 07 06
10 9 8 7 6 5 4 3 2 1

ISBN 1 406 20435 8 (paperback)
10 09 08 07 06
10 9 8 7 6 5 4 3 2 1

**British Library Cataloguing in
Publication Data**
Townsend, John
Pox, pus & plague : a history of disease. -
Differentiated ed. - (A painful history of medicine)
616'.009
A full catalogue record for this book is available
from the British Library.

This levelled text is a version of *Freestyle: A Painful
History of Medicine: Pox, Pus and Plague*

Acknowledgements
Alamy Images pp. **16** (Medical on Line), **50–51**
(image100); Art Directors and Trip pp. **7**, **13**, **21**
(Helene Rogers); Bridgeman Art Library pp. **14**
(Alinari Osterreichische Nationalbibliothek,
Vienna, Austria), **16–17** (Guildhall Library,
Corporation of London, UK), **19**, **22** (Private
Collection), **36** (Archives Charmet); (Chicago
Department of Water Management) pp. **24–25**;
Corbis pp. **6** (Lester V Bergman), **8** (Historical
Picture Archive), **11** (Mark Peterson), **12**
(Bettmann), **23** (Hulton-Deutsch Collection), **24**,
26–27, **30–31** (Bettmann), **32** (CDC/PHIL), **35**
(Hulton-Deutsch Collection), **39** (Bettman),
42–43 (Phil Schermeister), **43** (Gideon Mandel),
47 (Children's Hospital & Medical Center),
48–49 (Reuters), **49** (Alan Hindle), **53**; Frank
Graham p. **9**; GettyImages/ PhotoDisc pp. **50**,
51; Hulton Archive pp. **38–39**; Kobal Collection
pp. **36–37**; Mary Evans Picture Library p. **28**;
Medical on Line pp. **10**, **19**, **20**, **29**, **33**, **34–35**,
40–41; Science Photo Library pp. **4–5**
(Custom Medical Stock Photo), **10–11** (Mauro
Fermariello), **14–15** (St Mary's Hospital Medical
School), **18** (John Walsh), **22–23** (Dr Klaus
Boller), **34** (Custom Medical Stock Photo), **41**
(St Mary's Hospital Medical School), **44** (R
Umesh Chandran), **44–45** (Andrew Syred), **45**
(Volker Steger), **46** (Colin Cuthbert); Wellcome
Library, London pp. **27**, **28**, **30**, **32–33**.

Cover photograph of woman in iron lung
reproduced with permission of Corbis/Bettmann

Every effort has been made to contact copyright
holders of any material reproduced in this book.
Any omissions will be rectified in subsequent
printings if notice is given to the publishers.

Disclaimer
All the Internet addresses (URLs) given in this
book were valid at the time of going to press.
However, due to the dynamic nature of the
Internet, some addresses may have changed, or
sites may have changed or ceased to exist since
publication. While the author and publishers
regret any inconvenience this may cause readers,
no responsibility for any such changes can be
accepted by either the author or the publishers.

The paper used to print this book comes from
sustainable resources.

Contents

Under attack   4

Ancient times   6

The Middle Ages   10

Epidemic   16

Secrets in the water   24

Great discoveries   32

Up to date   42

Find out more   52

Glossary   54

Index   56

Any words appearing in the text in bold,
like this, are explained in the glossary.
You can also look out for them in the Word
bank at the bottom of each page.

Under attack

On the defence

Our bodies have to fight diseases all the time. Tiny living things try to invade us. But the body has a defence. This is called an **immune system**. This attacks the tiny living things. It stops diseases.

Our bodies work well most of the time. Then we do not think about them much. When they go wrong we soon know. Diseases are bad news. Oozing boils and rotting flesh are nasty. Even the common cold is not very pleasant.

It is amazing our bodies do not go wrong more often. After all, they are always under attack.

Some rashes can spread fast if they are not treated.

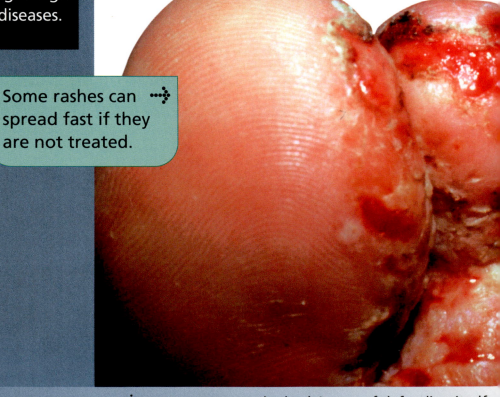

Word bank   **immune system**   the body's way of defending itself against diseases

Questions and answers

Doctors have always asked questions about diseases. Here are three of them:

1. *How do people catch diseases?*
2. *Why do some diseases spread so fast?*
3. *How can they be cured?*

Doctors have found answers to these questions. Now we can fight many diseases. But it has taken thousands of years of **pox, pus,** and **plagues** to learn how!

Find out later...

...which disease causes black vomit.

...what leprosy is.

...which diseases people fear today.

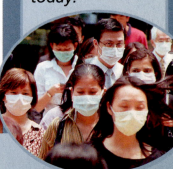

pus thick green or yellow liquid made by infected wounds. It often smells foul.

Ancient times

People catch diseases from each other. This is because we like to live together in large groups. We started living in large groups 10,000 years ago.

Spreading diseases

People catch diseases from their animals too. Animal food and **dung** attract insects and rats. They spread even more diseases. When people move to new areas they can pass diseases on to other groups of people.

Word bank   **virus**   tiny living thing that breaks into the body's cells and causes a disease

Egyptians

The ancient Egyptians lived 4,000 years ago. They thought the body could get blocked and this caused diseases.

They unblocked the body in a number of ways. They tried to **vomit** or be sick. They ate **senna**. This is made from the seeds of the cassia tree. It helps you go to the toilet. They also cut themselves. They did this to bleed away the disease.

Viruses

The Egyptians thought that blood could carry diseases. They were right! One thousand viruses can live in one red blood **cell**!

This is a 3,000-year-old Egyptian mummy. There are marks on the face. They were probably left by the **smallpox** disease.

cell   tiny unit that makes up all animal and plant tissue

Greeks in the past

The ancient Greeks and Romans had **plagues**. Plagues are deadly diseases. They spread very quickly over a wide area.

Around 2,400 years ago there was a plague in Athens in Greece. The plague killed a third of the people.

Unhealthy places

Greeks saw marshy or very wet lowlands as unhealthy. They were right! **Mosquitoes** breed in marshy lowlands. These insects spread **malaria**. Malaria is another deadly disease.

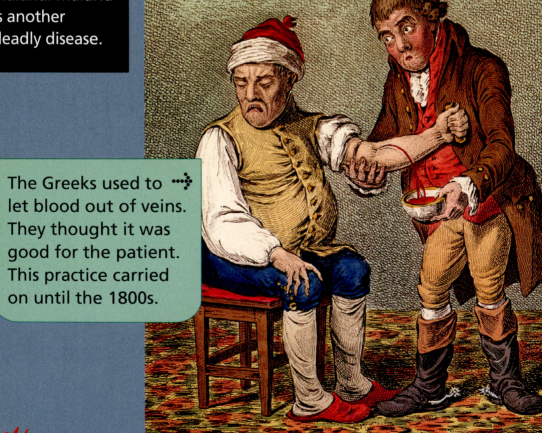

The Greeks used to let blood out of veins. They thought it was good for the patient. This practice carried on until the 1800s.

Word bank

mosquito   tiny insect that sucks blood from animals and people, and can spread diseases

Romans in the past

The Romans knew where diseases came from. They came from bad air and bad water. They also came from **marshy** land, **sewage,** or waste. The Romans built public toilets. They flushed away their sewage.

The Romans kept themselves clean. But they still got **worms**. Worms live inside people's bodies. They are caught from food that is poorly cooked.

Roman toilets got rid of waste safely. The toilets were also good meeting places!

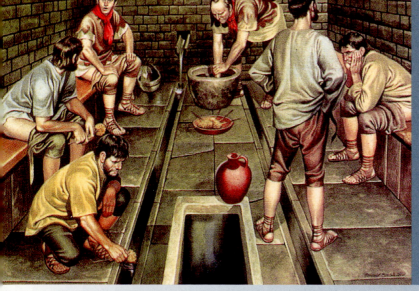

malaria disease that causes fevers and chills, spread by mosquito bites

The Middle Ages

The **Middle Ages** was a time in history. It was about 500 to 1,500 years ago. In the Middle Ages, people did not know what caused diseases. They did not know how to cure them. They had some odd ideas!

Beliefs

If people were sick, they thought they were being punished for being bad. No one had any sympathy for the sick.

Oozing pus

" When **scrofula** develops, cut the swellings, so that **pus** comes out. "

Roger de Salerno, a doctor in the 14th **century**.

Urine samples are still tested for diseases.

Many people got scrofula in the Middle Ages. It caused a swelling in the victim's neck.

Word bank   **century**   hundred years

Finding a cure

Doctors tried to cure illness with magic or plants. Many monks grew plants. They sold them as drugs. Witches also used plants to treat diseases.

Doctors looked at the colour of patients' **urine**. They did this to see if they could find out what was wrong with them. Doctors look at urine today. But the science is more exact now!

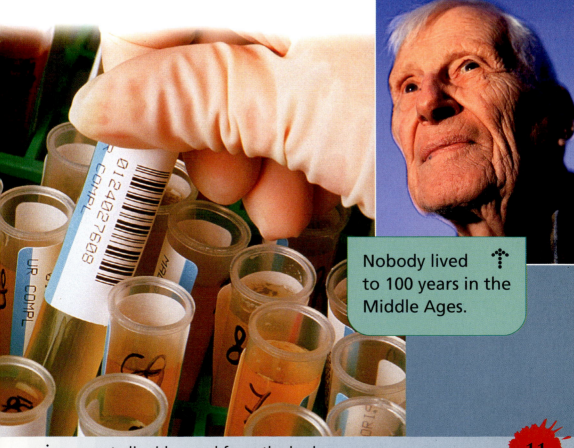

Nobody lived to 100 years in the Middle Ages.

urine   waste liquid passed from the body, usually pale yellow

The Black Death

In the 1300s people lived in fear. They worried that the Black Death or **plague** would strike them.

The Black Death was caused by tiny living things. They are called **bacteria**. Fleas spread the bacteria. The fleas drank the blood of diseased rats. Then they bit people, cats, and dogs. Then the disease passed into the victims.

The Plague

A plague began in China. Travellers from Europe visited China. They caught the disease. Then they took it to Europe. There it killed 65 million people.

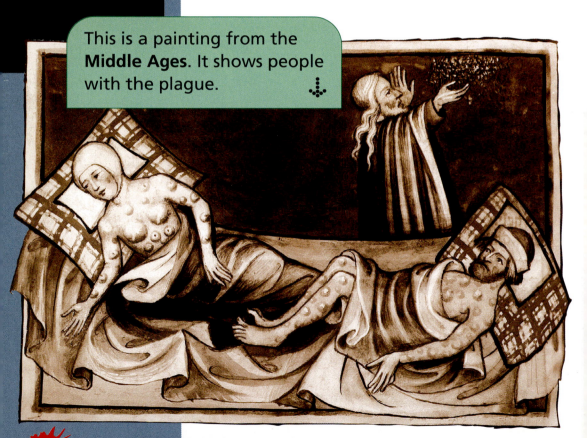

This is a painting from the **Middle Ages**. It shows people with the plague.

Word bank   **bacteria**   tiny living things. Some can cause diseases.

Lumps and blood

Victims of the plague had a grim death. They got headaches and aching joints. They got a **fever** and **vomited**. Their **glands** swelled and were painful. The swollen glands were called **buboes**. This led to the name bubonic plague.

There were other types of plague. These were spread by sneezes or even clothes. The **saliva** or spit of these victims was full of blood. The slimy saliva dribbled from their mouths and noses.

Huge lumps

It began with swellings in the groin and armpit. Some of these were as big as apples and some were shaped like eggs.

Boccaccio, an Italian writer (1313–1375).

Fleas on rats carried the plague.

gland   part of the body that makes chemicals

Old and new worlds

In the **Middle Ages** people began to explore the world. Sailors set out to find new lands. They brought back lots of new things. They also brought back new **bacteria**. These bacteria caused new diseases.

People lived in the new lands. They caught diseases from the sailors. They even died from the common cold. They had no **immunity**. This means their bodies could not fight diseases.

Sick sailors

Sailors did not just get sea-sick. They fell ill with lots of other things. Insect bites, bad food, and bacteria killed sailors.

In the Middle Ages life on a ship was not healthy.

Word bank   diet   type of food eaten

Poor food

Food can cause people to get very ill. Sailors could be out at sea for many months. They ate a very bad **diet**. Often they only had ship's biscuits.

A poor diet could cause a disease called **scurvy**. The skin went black with **ulcers** or open sores. Teeth fell out and the gums rotted. Victims often went mad and died. But scurvy is easy to cure. You just need to eat fruit.

Scurvy makes gums painful and swollen.

Limeys

A lack of **vitamin** C causes scurvy. You find vitamin C in fresh fruit, like limes. British sailors took lime juice on their ships. Then the sailors did not get scurvy. They got the nickname "limeys".

Epidemic

Some diseases are very hard to stop. They spread out of control. A disease like this is called an **epidemic**.

The 1600s

The 1600s were not a good time for London, England. In 1665 the **plague** struck. Within a few months 55,000 people had died. That was a fifth of the people who lived in London.

The great plague

Doctors could easily catch the plague. They wore leather gowns and masks to protect themselves (above). But this outfit did not keep out fleas.

Word bank   **epidemic**   when a disease spreads quickly over a wide area

On the move

In 1665 some cloth was sent from London to Eyam. This is a village in Derbyshire, England. There were fleas on the cloth. They were **infected** with the plague. Half of the villagers had died in a few weeks.

In 1666 the plague was still in London. Then there was a huge fire. It burnt down much of the city. The fire killed the rats and their fleas. It stopped the plague.

Graveyard

Mass graves from 1665 have been found. They show lots of people were buried together in a hurry. The bodies were all piled in at once.

The great fire of London burnt down 13,000 houses in four days.

mass grave   huge grave where lots of people were buried together

Yellow fever

Yellow fever was a deadly disease. Ships carried yellow fever across the world. Yellow fever is a **virus. Mosquitoes** bit sailors. They gave them the virus. Other mosquitoes bit **infected** sailors. They carried the disease to other people.

Yellow fever made the stomach bleed. The blood made the juices in the stomach turn black.

Blood thirsty

Mosquitoes stab the skin to feed on blood (below). As they drink, they pass viruses into the victim's blood. That is how yellow fever spreads.

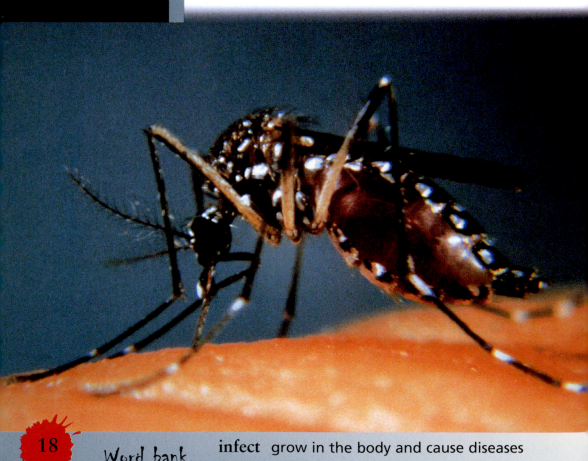

Word bank   **infect** grow in the body and cause diseases

Black vomit

Yellow fever turned the skin bright yellow. This was because it damaged the liver.

It had other nasty effects too. The writing below tells us about them.

*"Her tongue and lips were dark and cracked. Blood oozed from the mouth and nose. The black **vomit** was the worst thing. It was as black as ink."*

Black vomit was a sign of yellow fever.

Vaccine at last

There is a **vaccine** for yellow fever now. It was first used in the 1930s. A vaccine is a type of medicine that helps the body defend itself against the disease. This girl, in the picture above, is being protected against yellow fever in India.

vaccine medicine that makes the body defend itself against a disease

Measles

Measles is a **virus**. It can be spread by sneezing. It can be spread by sharing cups or spoons. It causes a rash, cough, and **fever**. It can even kill a person.

The 1800s

In the 1800s, measles spread across the world. Millions of people became ill. Some of them died.

A measles rash can be itchy.

Word bank   **fever**   very high body temperature

Leprosy

Leprosy is caused by **bacteria**. It spreads through coughing and sneezing. People with leprosy get sores and swellings. This can destroy the face. It can make the victim blind. Leprosy can make parts of the body lose feeling.

There are still many cases of leprosy. Most of these are in South-east Asia, Africa, and South America.

Progress

- In 1873, leprosy bacteria were first found.
- In the 1940s, an **antibiotic** was found. This type of medicine helped to kill the leprosy bacteria.

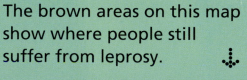

The brown areas on this map show where people still suffer from leprosy.

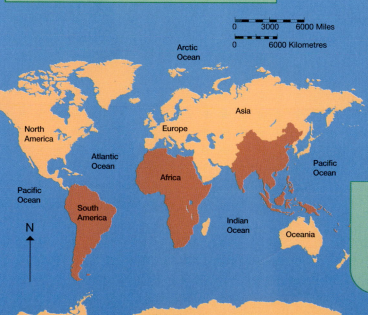

0 3000 6000 Miles
0 6000 Kilometres

Arctic Ocean

Asia

North America

Europe

Atlantic Ocean

Pacific Ocean

Africa

Pacific Ocean

South America

N

Indian Ocean

Oceania

Antarctica

Today, leprosy can be cured, if people can pay for the right drugs.

antibiotic medicine that kills harmful bacteria

Flu

Flu **epidemics** do not just kill the old and weak. They can kill healthy people too.

The 1900s

Less than a hundred years ago, flu killed millions of people. When World War 1 ended, many people moved around. A deadly type of flu was moving too. This flu killed young, healthy people. Half of its victims were aged between 20 and 40 years.

Did you know?

Flu causes **fever**, headache, and chills. It gives you a runny nose, sore throat, and coughs. It makes you feel awful!

Many children died of flu in the 1800s.

Word bank

Fighting back

A tiny **virus** causes flu. In 1930, scientists built an **electron microscope**. Scientists could then see the flu virus. They found out about different types of flu. They made better **vaccines**. But viruses can change.

Scientists watch out for new types of flu. They have to make new vaccines to stop another flu epidemic.

American police in 1918 wore masks. This was to protect them from flu.

This is the flu virus. It can be seen under an electron microscope.

Killer flu

- In 1918 flu hit the United States.
- In October 1918, flu killed 195,000 Americans.
- In one day 851 people died in New York City.

electron microscope   microscope that uses electron beams to make images much larger

Secrets in the water

Everyone needs to drink water. But water can kill you. People thought that if water looked clean, it was safe to drink. They were wrong.

Causing a stink

The River Thames in London, England, was called the "Great Stink". In the 1850s human waste went into the river. The river was used for drinking water!

Cesspits

In the 1900s human waste was put into holes in the ground. These were called **cesspits**. But the waste seeped into the soil and into wells. This made drinking water unsafe.

Maxwell Street in Chicago was once a **slum** area. Animal **dung** was dumped in streets like this.

Word bank

typhoid disease caused by bacteria. Typhoid bacteria can be caught from food or water.

Chicago

A river flows through Chicago, United States. In the 1800s, people tipped their waste into it.

The people of Chicago drank the river water. Diseases, like **typhoid** and **cholera,** spread quickly. In the end big pipes called sewers (below) were built. They carried the **sewage** away. Then the river in Chicago was clean and safe.

Animal waste

In the 1870s, there were more pigs than people in some parts of London. That was a lot of **dung**. It clogged up the streets and drained into the water supply.

cholera disease that causes very bad stomach upsets and can kill

Typhoid

Typhoid fever begins like flu. Then a red rash appears on the chest and back. Victims get **diarrhoea** and a dry mouth. They can be dead in a few weeks.

In the 1800s, doctors did not know that **bacteria** caused typhoid. People were catching it from dirty water. Today typhoid can be treated with **antibiotics**. These are medicines that can kill harmful bacteria.

Easily spread

Typhoid is spread in drinking water. You can get it from unwashed hands too. Flies can carry typhoid from **sewage** on to food.

Mary Mallon was called "Typhoid Mary". This was because she spread typhoid. She was put into an **institution** like this until she died.

Word bank   **diarrhoea**   when waste is liquid and you need to use the toilet often

A dangerous lady

Some people can carry typhoid and not be affected. They can give it to others.

Mary Mallon was a cook. She worked in a house in New York in the early 1900s. Six people in the house caught typhoid. Doctors found Mary was a carrier. She was told to keep away from kitchens. Later, 20 people caught typhoid in a hospital. Mary Mallon was the cook. The police locked her up.

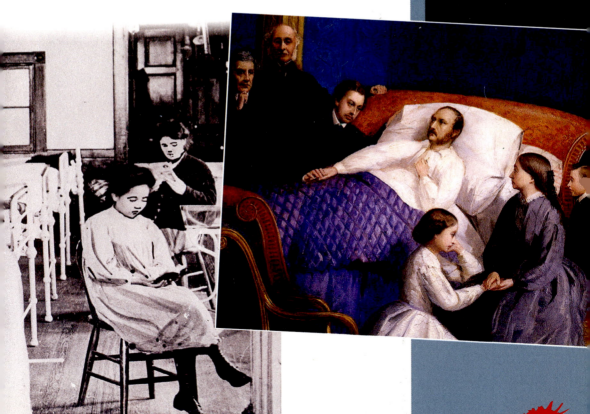

institution   type of hospital where people are not allowed to leave

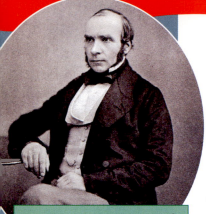

Cholera

When people have **cholera**, they get very bad **diarrhoea**. They are also very sick. In the past doctors could not treat cholera. Many people died of it.

Today, we can cure cholera. But doctors have to treat it quickly. They have to put liquids and salts back into the body. Then the patient needs to take **antibiotics**. These kill the **bacteria**.

This is Doctor John Snow. He proved that cholera is carried in dirty water.

This cartoon shows the River Thames as a father. He is bringing his children **Diptheria**, Cholera, and **Scrofula** to London.

Recent cholera epidemics

- **1971:** Bangladesh, Asia – 6,500 deaths
- **1991:** Peru, South America – 3,000 deaths
- **1994:** Rwanda, Africa – 20,000 deaths.

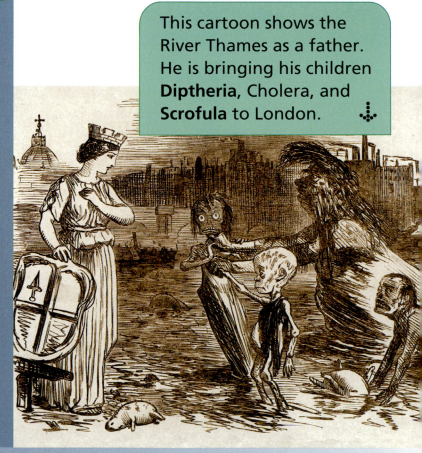

Word bank scrofula   disease causing swellings, common in the Middle Ages

A discovery

John Snow was a British doctor. He was sure people caught cholera from water. But other doctors did not agree. Everyone thought cholera was spread in smelly air. He changed their ideas.

A mother washed her baby's nappy in a London well. It was 1854. Cholera broke out and 616 people died. John Snow proved that they all drank water from the same well. He showed that cholera was spread in water.

Dirty water

We need clean water for drinking. Many poor countries still do not have this. People who live in those countries are at risk of cholera.

These are cholera bacteria. They live in dirty water.

diptheria   disease causing a high fever and making your throat so swollen that breathing is difficult

Polio

Polio is a **virus**. It has killed and **disabled** many people. Children often caught it. They got it from swimming pools and drinking water.

Many polio victims died. This was because they were unable to breathe. Other victims could not walk anymore. They had to use crutches.

Iron lung

An iron lung is a machine. It was first made in 1928. Polio sufferers lay inside it and a pump helped them to breathe.

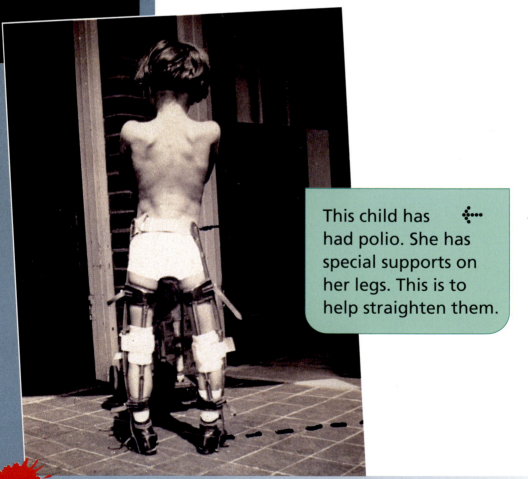

This child has had polio. She has special supports on her legs. This is to help straighten them.

Word bank   **disable**   cause a problem that affects someone's way of life

War

Franklin Roosevelt was President of the United States in the 1930s. He caught polio as an adult. Roosevelt did a lot to help learn more about the disease.

Jonas Salk and Albert Sabin were scientists. They worked on a polio **vaccine** for over ten years. They made one in 1955. The United States became free from polio in 1979.

Happy ending

In 2001, 575 million children were given the polio vaccine. That year, there were only 500 cases of polio in the world.

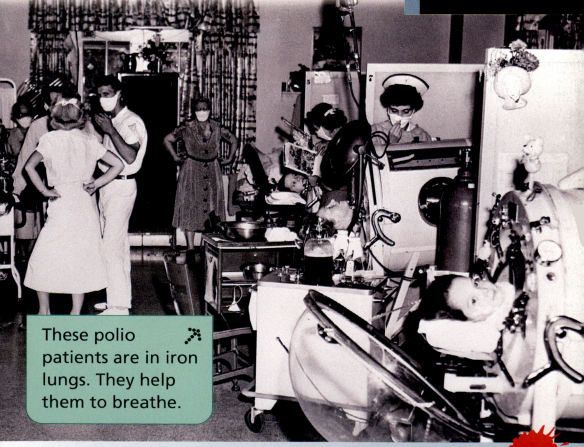

These polio patients are in iron lungs. They help them to breathe.

vaccine   medicine that makes the body defend itself against a disease

Great discoveries

Some people have made very important discoveries. They have helped us fight diseases. Edward Jenner was one of those people. He was born in the 1700s. He found a **vaccine** against **smallpox**.

Smallpox

Smallpox was a terrible disease. Victims got nasty blisters and a high **fever**. A third of the people who caught it died.

This girl is covered in smallpox blisters. They leave scars called **pockmarks**.

No signs

Smallpox was very easy to catch. People had smallpox before they felt ill. They did not know they were giving the disease to others.

This is a cartoon from 1802. It shows that vaccination turns patients into animals!

Word bank   **pockmark**   round scar left on the skin after a pox disease

Edward Jenner

Milkmaids did not catch smallpox. Edward Jenner noticed this. They only got cowpox. This is a mild form of smallpox. They only got blisters on their hands.

Jenner injected some **pus** from the cowpox blisters into a **volunteer**. Then Jenner gave him smallpox. He became ill. After a few days he got better. Jenner had found a vaccine against smallpox.

Doctor Edward Jenner was English.

Wiped out

In the 1970s there was a big effort to get rid of smallpox. People across the world were given the vaccine. In 1980 smallpox was wiped out.

volunteer   someone who offers to take part in something

Louis Pasteur

Louis Pasteur (1822–1895) was a French scientist. He had the idea that there are tiny living things, called **bacteria.** He found that bacteria can live everywhere. Pasteur was sure that bacteria could get into our bodies. They could cause diseases. He wanted to find ways of killing bacteria in the body.

Big ideas

Pasteur knew there was a vaccine for smallpox. He thought there would be a vaccine for all diseases.

Word bank   **pasteurization**   heating a liquid, like milk or orange juice, to kill bacteria

Anthrax

Anthrax is a disease that kills animals. It can pass to humans in wool, cloth, and leather. Pasteur began working with anthrax bacteria. He found out that one kind of bacteria could attack and kill another kind. He tried this with anthrax. It worked. Pasteur had made a **vaccine** for the disease anthrax.

Milk

Today our milk is free from bacteria. It is safe to drink. We heat it to kill the bacteria. This is **pasteurization**. We have Louis Pasteur to thank for this.

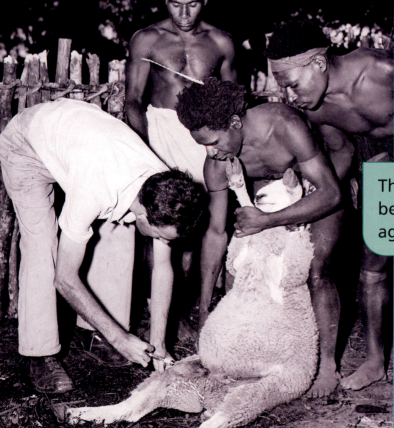

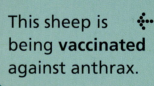

This sheep is being **vaccinated** against anthrax.

vaccinate   give someone a vaccine

Rabies

Rabies is a deadly **virus**. People can get bitten by an **infected** animal. Then they catch it. Rabies starts with pain, **fever**, and headache. It leads to shaking and a fear of water. Then it causes madness, **coma**, and death.

Louis Pasteur made a **vaccine**. It worked on animals. But would it help humans?

This dog has rabies.

Danger

Dogs with rabies are very dangerous. Pasteur wanted to collect a dog's **saliva**. Then he could study the rabies virus. Members of his team had to hold a dog down (above). Then he collected the saliva.

Word bank **coma** like a deep sleep, usually caused by injury or diseases

Risk

In 1885 a dog with rabies bit a boy, called Joseph. Joseph would have died in agony. He was taken to Louis Pasteur. Pasteur tried out his vaccine on him. This was a risk. Luckily Joseph became well again. Pasteur then knew his vaccine worked.

Since then, many people's lives have been saved from rabies.

Did you know?

People still die from rabies. This happens if they do not get the vaccine in time. Each year, around 50,000 people in the world die from rabies.

saliva   spit and liquid inside the mouth

Deadly lung disease

Tuberculosis (TB) is a serious disease. It was feared well into the 1900s. It affects the lungs. Victims get a bad cough and **fever**. They are tired and do not feel like eating. People with TB often cough up blood too.

Killer disease

In the 1700s and 1800s, TB killed millions of people. It was the main cause of death in Europe and the United States.

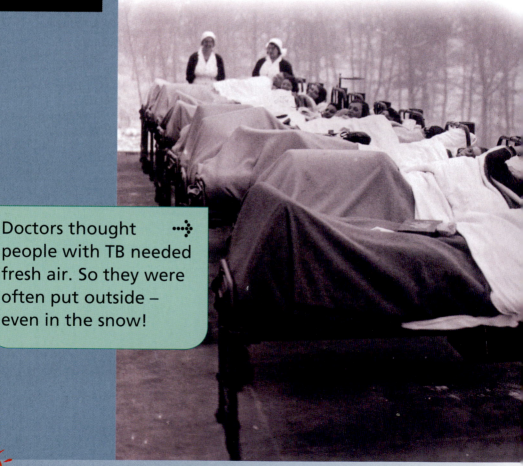

Doctors thought people with TB needed fresh air. So they were often put outside – even in the snow!

Word bank

cholera   disease that causes very bad stomach upsets and can kill

Robert Koch

Robert Koch was a German doctor. He and his team knew that **bacteria** caused TB. But they had to find which type. In 1882, after a long search, Koch found it. The next year he discovered the bacteria that caused **cholera**. Then scientists could make the **vaccines**. These would protect people from TB and cholera.

Robert Koch's work saved millions of lives. In 1905 he received the **Nobel Prize.**

TB today

TB is still a danger. It kills over a million people each year. It can be caught in damp and crowded places.

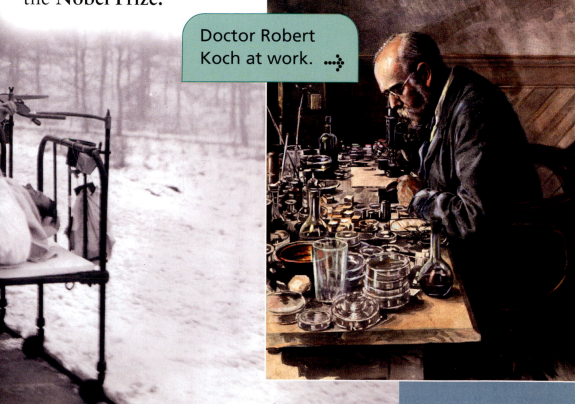

Doctor Robert Koch at work. ···>

Nobel Prize   prize given for very special work

Penicillin

Penicillin is a wonder drug! This was the world's first **antibiotic**. An antibiotic is a type of drug. It can kill harmful **bacteria**.

Doctors began using penicillin in the 1940s. Since then, it has saved millions of lives.

Pneumonia

Pneumonia is a disease. It makes breathing difficult. Many children used to die from it. Now it is treated with penicillin. Today most children survive it.

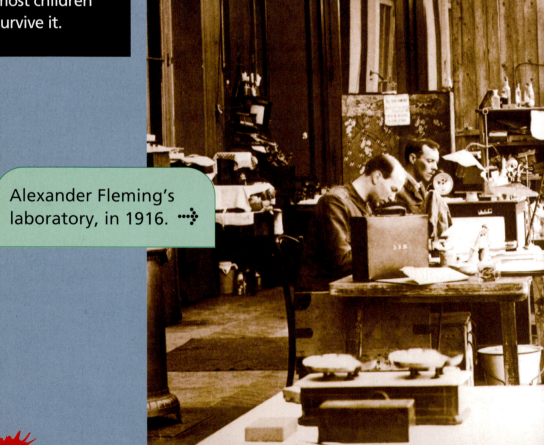

Alexander Fleming's laboratory, in 1916. ⋯⋗

Word bank   **bacteria**   tiny living things. Some can cause diseases.

Alexander Fleming

In 1928, Alexander Fleming left the lid off a dish of bacteria. This was a mistake. He found **mould** growing on the dish. He was amazed at what he saw. The mould had killed the bacteria. This mould was called *penicillium*.

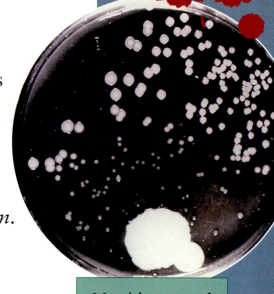

Other scientists worked on *penicillium*. They found that it could fight all kinds of diseases. *Penicillium* mould was made into the drug penicillin.

Mould grew over Fleming's dish.

Growing mould

Scientists needed a lot of *penicillium* mould. They wanted to make it into a drug and test it. They grew mould in many places.

mould   type of fungus that grows in damp places

Up to date

We have learnt a lot about diseases in the last 30 years. But there is still plenty for us to learn.

HIV

In the late 1970s, a new **virus** appeared. It was first noticed in young men. They were unable to fight **infection**. The new virus was called HIV.

HIV is not like other viruses. It is not spread by coughing and sneezing. You can only catch HIV from body fluids. Blood and **semen** are body fluids.

An AIDS patient in San Francisco, United States.

Word bank   semen   fluid that contains sperm

AIDS

The HIV virus sometimes develops into an illness, called AIDS. This stands for Acquired Immune Deficiency Syndrome.

A patient with AIDS cannot fight infections. There is still no cure for AIDS. Millions of people have died from it.

AIDS orphans

In Africa, the parents of 23 million children have died of AIDS.

By 2010, 40 million children in the world will be **orphans** because of AIDS. These children (below) are orphans. AIDS has killed their parents.

orphan   someone, especially a child, whose parents are dead

Parasites

Many creatures live in or on our bodies. Most do not hurt us. But there are some that do harm us. They live or feed on us. They are called **parasites.**

Tapeworms and round **worms** are parasites. They can get inside us. This happens if we touch **infected** food, water, or animals. A billion people have these worms. They kill 20,000 people every year.

Just one bite

One type of mosquito injects tiny worm **larvae** into the blood. The worms grow and cause a disease called **elephantiasis**. This makes the legs swell up (below).

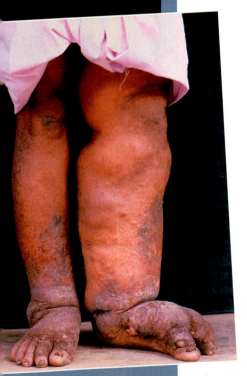

This is a tapeworm. Some can grow to over 10 metres (30 feet) long.

Word bank   **mosquito**   tiny insect that sucks blood from animals and people, and can spread diseases

Malaria

Malaria is like flu. It lasts up to 20 days. Sometimes it affects the kidneys or the brain. Then it can kill. Malaria is caused by a **virus**. A type of **mosquito** carries the virus. It bites someone. Then it passes the virus into the blood.

Today there are drugs that can treat malaria. Even so, it kills over a million people each year.

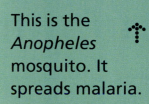

This is the *Anopheles* mosquito. It spreads malaria.

Did you know?

- Malaria is still the main cause of death in Africa.

- The young and old are at most risk of dying of malaria.

- Two children die of malaria every minute.

larva   very young form of a worm or an insect

Cancer

Cancer is the disease that people now fear the most. In richer countries a third of people will get cancer. Twenty per cent of these die of the disease.

There are many types of cancer. They all start when our body **cells** grow out of control. Cancer cells often form a growth or lump. This is called a **tumour**. Some cancers do not form tumours. **Leukaemia** is like this. It affects the blood.

These scientists are testing anti-cancer drugs.

Word bank   **leukaemia**   type of cancer that affects blood cells

Progress

Scientists are working hard to find a way to stop us from getting cancer. They are trying to find out what makes cells grow out of control. Then they hope to make **anti-cancer** drugs.

Now, doctors can usually treat cancer, if it is caught early. In the last 10 years the number of deaths from cancer has actually fallen.

Giant tumour

Marie Bell had stomach pains in 1999. She had a giant tumour. It was the size of a beach ball. Four doctors removed the tumour. It took them four hours to do it.

The dark area on this liver is a tumour. It is caused by cancer.

anti-cancer   something that prevents or fights cancer

Bird flu

Birds can catch a type of flu. Since 2004, there has been a flu **epidemic** in birds. It started in Vietnam. Vietnam is in Asia. The **virus** spread through hens in Asia. Nearly 5 million chickens were killed and buried.

People can catch this flu from birds. It often kills them. People are worried there could be a bird flu epidemic in humans.

Still not safe

Some diseases, like flu, can **adapt**. They can change so that drugs, like **antibiotics**, do not affect them. They can spread easily too. A new virus can cross the world in a few hours on a plane.

These men were burying chickens in the bird flu outbreak in Vietnam 2004.

Word bank   **adapt**   change to fit in with new conditions

SARS

A new disease broke out in China, in 2002. It was called **SARS**. People were scared that it might be a bad epidemic. In Ontario, Canada there was a big SARS scare. People were not allowed to travel. This was to stop the disease from spreading.

In fact, 8,098 people caught SARS in the world. Of these, 774 died.

Mad cow disease

There was a new brain disease in the 1990s. It mainly affected cows. Some people caught a similar disease. This was called new variant CJD. There is no cure yet. **Infected** people will die.

People in Hong Kong wore medical masks in the streets. This was to protect them from SARS.

SARS   Severe Acute Respiratory Syndrome. It affects the lungs and breathing.

49

Latest developments

There are still many health problems in the world. Scientists are working hard to try and find answers to them.

Ebola affects people in parts of Africa. It causes bleeding inside the body. The ebola **virus** kills over 75 per cent of its victims. This disease has no cure. But in 2004, scientists made some big steps. They hope this will lead to a safe **vaccine** soon.

Alzheimer's

Today people live longer. But old people still get Alzheimer's. This is when the brain no longer works properly. Scientists are working on new drugs. They may help to control Alzheimer's.

Many older people are healthy and active.

Word bank

ebola   disease that causes massive blood loss and a fast death

Breakthrough

There may be a vaccine against cancer soon. A team of British scientists have been working on this. They have made big steps in developing a vaccine against **leukaemia**. This is cancer of the blood. Doctors tested the vaccine on mice with the disease. They lived much longer.

We have won many battles against diseases. But the war is not over. We are now waiting for the next discovery.

Healthy bacteria

Most **bacteria** are useful. They help us break down our food, so our bodies can use it. They make important **vitamins**. These are chemicals that keep us healthy.

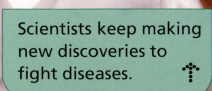

Scientists keep making new discoveries to fight diseases.

vitamin   chemical needed by the body for good health

Find out more

Books

Groundbreakers: Alexander Fleming, Steve Parker (Heinemann Library, 2001)

Nasty Bugs and Ghastly Medicine: A Painful History of Childhood, John Townsend (Raintree, 2006)

You Wouldn't Want To Be Sick In The 16th Century! Diseases You'd Rather Not Catch, Kathryn Sencor (Franklin Watts, 2002)

Using the Internet

The Internet can tell you more about medicine through the ages. You can use a search engine, such as www.yahooligans.com.
Type in keywords such as:

- bubonic plague
- tuberculosis
- medicine + Nobel Prize

Search tips

There are billions of pages on the Internet. It can be difficult to find what you are looking for.

These search tips will help you find useful websites more quickly:

- Know exactly what you want to find out about.
- Use two to six keywords in a search. Put the most important word first.
- Only use names of people, places, or things.

Where to search

Search engine
A search engine looks through millions of website pages. It lists all the sites that match the words in the search box. You will find the best matches are at the top of the list, on the first page.

Search directory
A person instead of a computer has sorted a search directory. You can search by keyword or subject and browse through the different sites. It is like looking through books on a library shelf.

Glossary

adapt change to fit in with new conditions

antibiotic medicine that kills harmful bacteria

anti-cancer something that prevents or fights cancer

bacteria tiny living things. Some can cause diseases.

bubo swollen area in the groin or armpit

cell tiny unit that makes up all animal and plant tissue

century hundred years

cesspit hole dug to hold waste and sewage

cholera disease that causes very bad stomach upsets and can kill

coma like a deep sleep, usually caused by injury or diseases

diarrhoea when waste is liquid and you need to use the toilet often

diet type of food eaten

diptheria disease causing a high fever and making your throat so swollen that breathing is difficult

disable cause a problem that affects someone's way of life

dung waste matter (manure) from an animal

ebola disease that causes massive blood loss and a fast death

electron microscope microscope that uses electron beams to make images much larger

elephantiasis huge swelling of an arm or leg caused by a type of worm

epidemic when a disease spreads quickly over a wide area

fever very high body temperature

gland part of the body that makes chemicals

immune system the body's way of defending itself against diseases

immunity the body's defence against diseases

infect grow in the body and cause diseases

infection disease that spreads easily

institution type of hospital where people are not allowed to leave

larva very young form of a worm or an insect

leukaemia type of cancer that affects blood cells

malaria disease that causes fevers and chills, spread by mosquito bites

marshy very wet land

mass grave huge grave where lots of people were buried together

Middle Ages period of history between about AD 500 and 1500

mosquito tiny insect that sucks blood from animals and people, and can spread diseases

mould type of fungus that grows in damp places

Nobel Prize prize given for very special work

orphan someone, especially a child, whose parents are dead

parasite living thing that lives or feeds on other living things, often harming them

pasteurization heating a liquid, like milk or orange juice, to kill bacteria

penicillin antibiotic drug made from a mould

plague deadly disease that spreads quickly

pneumonia disease of the lungs that makes it difficult to breathe

pockmark round scar left on the skin after a pox disease

pox any disease that causes a rash of spots that are filled with pus

pus thick green or yellow liquid made by infected wounds. It often smells foul.

saliva spit and fluid inside the mouth

SARS Severe Acute Respiratory Syndrome. It affects the lungs and breathing.

scrofula disease causing swellings, common in the Middle Ages

scurvy disease caused by a lack of vitamin C

semen fluid that contains sperm

senna powder made from the seeds of a cassia tree

sewage waste and dirty water from the toilet

slum group of houses in a city that are dirty, damp, and crowded

smallpox infectious disease. It causes blisters all over the body.

tumour growth or swelling in the body that is not normal

typhoid disease caused by bacteria. Typhoid bacteria can be caught from food or water.

ulcer open sore, often filled with pus

urine waste liquid passed from the body, usually pale yellow

vaccinate give someone a vaccine

vaccine medicine that makes the body defend itself against a disease

virus tiny living thing that breaks into the body's cells and causes a disease

vitamin chemical needed by the body for good health

volunteer someone who offers to take part in something

vomit throw up

worm kind of living thing that sometimes lives off animals' bodies

yellow fever disease spread by mosquitoes. It causes fever, aching limbs, yellow skin, and black vomit.

Index

AIDS 42–43
Alzheimer's disease 50
ancient times 6–9
anthrax 35
antibiotics 21, 28, 40, 48
bacteria 12, 14, 21, 26, 28, 34, 35, 39, 40, 51
bird flu 48
Black Death 12–13
blood-letting 7, 8
cancer 46–47, 51
cholera 25, 28–29, 39
common cold 4, 14, 52
diarrhoea 26, 28
diet, poor 15
ebola 50
Egyptians, ancient 7
electron microscopes 23
elephantiasis 44
epidemics 16–23, 28, 29, 30, 48
Fleming, Alexander 40, 41
flu 11, 22–23, 48
Greeks and Romans 8–9

HIV virus 42, 43
immune system 4, 42, 43
iron lungs 30, 31
Jenner, Edward 32–33
Koch, Robert 39
leprosy 21
leukaemia 46, 51
malaria 8, 45
measles 20
Middle Ages 10–15
new variant CJD 49
parasites 44
Pasteur, Louis 34, 35, 36, 37
penicillin 40
penicillium mould 41
plagues 8, 9, 12–13, 16–17
pneumonia 40
polio 30–31
rabies 36–37
SARS 49
scrofula 10
scurvy 15

sewage 9, 24, 25, 26
smallpox 7, 32–33, 34
spreading diseases 5, 6, 12, 14, 16, 17, 18, 20, 21, 22, 26, 32, 42, 48, 49
tuberculosis (TB) 38–39
tumours 46, 47
typhoid 25, 26–27
urine samples 10, 11
vaccines 19, 20, 23, 31, 32, 33, 35, 36, 37, 39, 51
viruses 6, 18, 23, 42, 43, 52
water-borne diseases 24–31
worms 9, 44
yellow fever 18–19